A special gift for

_____

With love from

_____

Date

_____

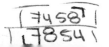

This gift edition is comprised of excerpts from
Honey, They Shrunk My Hormones

Honey, They Shrunk My Hormones

...nor and Insight
...n the Trenches of Midlife

...aron Chandler Loveless

Our purpose at Howard Publishing is to:
- *Increase faith* in the hearts of growing Christians
- *Inspire holiness* in the lives of believers
- *Instill hope* in the hearts of struggling people everywhere
  Because He's coming again!

Honey, They Shrunk My Hormones, Gift Edition © 2004 by Caron Chandler Loveless

All rights reserved. Printed in the United States of America

Published by Howard Publishing Co., Inc.
3117 North 7th Street, West Monroe, Louisiana 71291-2227
www.howardpublishing.com

04 05 06 07 08 09 10 11 12 13   10 9 8 7 6 5 4 3 2 1

Interior design by LinDee Loveland and Stephanie D. Walker
Compiled by Between the Lines
ISBN: 1-58229-365-1

Midlife seemed to come too soon.
I wish I had enjoyed my twenties and thirties
more, when I didn't have hot flashes, gray
hair, kids leaving home, low sex drive,
parents to care for, and wrinkles.

—Anne, 48

No one told us that to survive this
season of life, we would have to become
proficient in pharmacology, psychology,
biology, endocrinology, physiology,
cardiology, oncology, dermatology,
gynecology, ophthalmology, theology,
proctology, cosmetology, podiatry,
and naturopathy. Burdened with
a class load like this, no wonder
we sometimes get cranky.

If we went through the change
overnight, upon entering the menopausal
atmosphere, we would instantly
incinerate—since, some experts say,
a single hot flash is capable of raising a
woman's temperature seven or
eight degrees in mere seconds.

Midlife Awareness Quiz

1. A mammogram is:
   - ❑ A message from your mother delivered to your front door
   - ❑ A nutritional cracker designed for nursing moms
   - ❑ A cruel, but vital, test to measure a woman's threshold of pain

2. If a woman has her bunions removed, she has:
   - ❑ Asked her server to clear the remains of a fried Australian appetizer
   - ❑ Loosed her hair from its bun-dage
   - ❑ Just returned from a great shoe sale

I sought the LORD, and he answered me; . . .

4

3. The word *midlife* comes from:

   ❑ A novel by J. R. R. Tolkien

   ❑ A Midland, Texas, church choir newsletter

   ❑ A forty-something lexicographer in denial

4. The term *middle-age spread* refers to:

   ❑ A margarine product for people over forty

   ❑ A dude-ranch-turned-weight-loss clinic in central Wyoming

   ❑ The trunk region of a mature body storing excess fat to protect vital organs

. . . he delivered me from all my fears. —Psalm 34:4

Experts tell us that estrogen is involved
in at least *three hundred* bodily processes.
When it dips below levels the body has
come to expect for thirty years,
no wonder chaos ensues.

Everything from the brain to the hypothalamus gets confused, and with that goes the regulation of our sleep, temperature, appetite, libido, periods, and general sense of well-being.

I try not to focus on my physical self as much;
I try to look past the exterior.
In fact, I find myself much happier
when I keep the focus off myself and
put it more on others.

—June, 59

8

A plethora of books, medical
pamphlets, and Web sites dedicated
to women's health are available
to help you make informed decisions
about your body.

Compare natural and pharmaceutical options for relieving your symptoms. Make sure you have an OB/GYN you can trust— someone you're confident will give you the best medical counsel based on your one-of-a-kind needs. Or find a woman's hormonal health specialist.

I fought the idea of taking hormones
for a year because of horror stories. In that
time my skin dried up, my bones weakened,
and I became introverted and weird. I'm so
glad I started taking hormone replacements,
because I feel back to the real me.

—Martha, 49

11

No one would actually say, "You are no
longer a woman after menopause,"
but the fact that for decades we've had the
period-womanhood connection drilled into
our heads must at least *contribute*
to the confusion we feel as our
periods start to decrease.

Someone suggested looking at a failing womb like a piece of equipment that has outlived its usefulness. But when a blender breaks down or a purse wears out, we buy a new one.

Through the years our periods have brought everything from elation to irritation to inconvenience and despair. When they're gone, we won't miss the swelling, the edginess, or the ravenous appetites that came with them.

Perhaps what bothers us most about
menopause is that a part of us is,
let's face it . . . dying. Yet Christ's claim
on our lives transcends death,
since He calls us to live and serve with
Him every day at that higher place
where nothing ever dies.

In the past a "mortal womb" announced to the world, "She's rounding the bend, folks. She's heading into the home stretch. Her fruitful days are over." But this is a new day.

We have the potential to remain
vibrant and healthy well into old age.
And that's great, since the biblical
evidence is clear that our God Who Never
Changes is adamant about
His people bearing much fruit
at every stage of their lives.

Becoming a
Farsighted Female

1. Read Hebrews 12:1. Ask God: What things easily entangle me? What does the race You have marked out for me look like?

2. Read Romans 12:1. Ask God: How can I offer my body to You as a living, holy sacrifice? What would please You most?

Let us fix our eyes on Jesus, the author . . .

3. Read 1 Corinthians 2:9–10. Ask God: What do You want me to know about the future You've prepared for me? How can I love You more?

4. Read Isaiah 43:18–19. Ask God: What former things am I still holding on to? What is the new thing You want to do with me?

. . . and perfector of our faith. —Hebrews 12:2

One part of our bodies is closing up shop.
But this is just one storefront in the
thriving metropolis that is our life.
Let it be a sign, a commissioning,
a call to fling wide the door of our hearts
to a new, fertile place of influence
and productivity.

Instead of thinking, *Sorry, old girl. Time's up*, let's tell ourselves and one another, "OK, so our energies are needed elsewhere now. It's time to get a move on. Let's see where God wants us next."

Women who have passed through
menopause seem happier, more settled,
more resilient than the rest of us.
They've been through the fiery forties and
have come out on the other side. They
have more focus and a spiritual depth and
curiosity that is highly attractive.

I'm more secure and stronger about my opinions now, which is an adjustment for my husband. It doesn't really matter what people think of me. I have a goal to age gracefully and be an example to younger women who fight the physical aspects of aging.

—Suzie, 52

We're bewildered at how fast life is speeding by. Can we really be at this point already? We all get depressed and weird and lash out and have irrational fears that we've never felt before. Sometimes we isolate ourselves and don't even realize we're doing it.

Simply being together helps.
Gathering in one room, confronting our
issues aloud, seeing ourselves in others—
these things have a mystical way
of easing our anxiety and
making midlife seem doable.

There is a time for everything, and a season for every activity under heaven:

a time to be born
       and a time to die,

a time to plant
       and a time to uproot, . . .

a time to tear down
       and a time to build,

a time to weep
       and a time to laugh, . . .

a time to scatter stones
       and a time to gather them,

a time to embrace
and a time to refrain, . . .

a time to keep
and a time to throw away, . . .

a time to be silent
and a time to speak. . . .

[God] has made everything beautiful in its time.

—Ecclesiastes 3:1–7, 11

Women, especially maturing ones,
are world renowned for singing the
birthday blues. Every once in a while, a guy
might pipe in with a lament about his age;
but for the most part, we girls have
a monopoly on the market.
It seems we just can't get past the numbers.

I went through a huge crisis of grieving my fading youthfulness. Now I'm on the other side of it, and I truly love my life. The pressure is gone to look good for others. It's so freeing! I have only one true purpose now: to grow closer to Jesus.

—June, 59

29

Why are we so ashamed of our age?

Where does this attitude come from?

We don't feel this way

about the ages of other things.

In certain "acceptable areas," old is beautiful, valuable, honorable. So why don't we apply those adjectives to ourselves? Why do we squirm when someone asks our age? Why do we leave the age line blank on questionnaires? Why are we relieved to learn someone is older than us?

Oh Lord,

You are truly the God Who Never Changes. You're also the God of all seasons. We know that. We've seen that. You made us. You know our

Jesus Christ is the same . . .

frames. Help us to see Your purpose in this new and confusing stage in our lives. Help us to make some sense of it. Help us to trust You in it. And help us to make You proud.

. . . yesterday and today and forever. —Hebrews 13:8

Even if the whole earth worships
at the temple of youth, do we—
and millions of other smart, seasoned,
spiritual women like us—
really have to be age-a-phobic?

I love my age! I know where
I'm creative and what I'm gifted to do.
I also know what areas and situations
are "not me" and lead to frustration.

—Susan, 49

35

Putting the Crunch on Those Numbers

Don't let your birthday sneak up on you. Mark your calendar and prepare to celebrate.

- Spend part of the day enjoying yourself—by yourself. Do something you like to do but don't get the chance to do often.

- Call someone who would not expect to hear from you and tell them how they've made an impact on your life.

May the righteous be glad and rejoice before God; . . . .

- Write out three personal goals you'd like to accomplish by your next birthday.

- Be bold and plan your own birthday party!

- Record your personal history.

. . . may they be happy and joyful. —Psalm 68:3

Everyone knows a mammogram is a rite
of passage, a coming-of-middle-age
must-do; and when a woman gets one,
she becomes one of "them." The longer
she puts it off, the longer she can trick
herself into thinking she's younger
than all those other women her age.

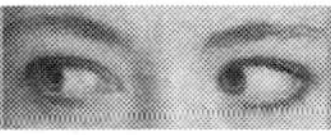

My first mammogram was so traumatic
and painful that after it was over,
I dropped to my knees and fainted.
The technician said
she'd never seen anyone do that before.

—Julie, 39

39

If there is any certainty

about midlife, it's that we now face

plenty of uncertainty.

When it was time for my first mammogram,

my mother was so worried about

how I'd feel that she offered to go with me.

But the whole experience

was a piece of cake.

—Shirley, 40

41

Strategies for Mammogram Procrastinators

- Try to get at the root of why you're procrastinating.

- Talk to at least five women who have had mammograms. Ask for tips to make the experience easier and get recommendations for the best imaging center in your area.

- Read the most current literature you can find on mammography.

She is clothed with strength and dignity; ...

- Give yourself a deadline. Make an appointment, and don't cancel! Ask a friend or family member to keep you accountable or, better yet, go with you.

- Talk with a nurse, doctor, or even a breast-cancer patient.

- Do it for someone you love.

. . . she can laugh at the days to come. —Proverbs 31:25

Middle age—for all the hype
about its treacherous, untried territories—
may just prove to be a fair,
hospitable land.

Once you get past a certain number

on a scale, it's easy to live

in denial about how

bad things really are.

Much has been said and written about
learning to accept our bodies, about loving
ourselves as we are. This is a good
principle. But there's too much evidence
about the damaging downsides of weight
gain to feel good about continuing to
pamper a porky, puffy person.

Too little sleep, too much stress,
and too much junk food in my twenties and
thirties have caused my body to age quicker.
I used to feel I could push myself
to keep going nonstop. Now I feel tired
and drained when I don't take care of myself.

—Martha, 49

47

If such great care was taken in Old
Testament times to build and maintain
God's tabernacle, how much more
should we care for our bodies,
which are God's living, holy temples?

We should be kind to ourselves, yes, and never judgmental or Pharisaical about anyone else's eating habits or body type. But we also need to love ourselves enough to dig up the emotional (or medical) roots that keep us trapped in habitual, negative food patterns year after year.

Midlife Awareness Quiz

1. When a woman is in menopause, she is:
   - ❏ Taking an afternoon nap
   - ❏ Taking a break from the Dictaphone
   - ❏ Free to do whatever she wants—any day of the month—for the rest of her life

2. The abbreviation HRT stands for:
   - ❏ Handsome Research Technician
   - ❏ Humor Replacement Therapy
   - ❏ Hoping for a Reduction in Temperature

He who began a good work in you . . .

3. When someone says she has an empty nest, she really means:

- ❏ A zero-balance retirement account
- ❏ The post atop the mast of a ship
- ❏ Clean, quiet housing for dazed and recovering parents

4. The best definition of a hot flash is:

- ❏ A popular Web site for late-breaking news
- ❏ The time between listing your teen's chores and his or her disappearance
- ❏ A single surge of power reported to burn three hundred calories per second and heat the entire town of Hooterville for fifteen minutes

. . . will carry it to completion. —Philippians 1:6

Not only can a woman in the throes of midlife develop overactive glands and follicles—she can also get male-pattern baldness; a bulging midriff; and her face, chest, and back can expand to more masculine proportions.

In the event this whole hair thing gets
really out of hand, you will have no
recourse but to join the millions
of baby-booming women who laser,
wax, or pay total strangers to shock them
in the face with electric needles
on a monthly basis.

I was in the car with my ten-year-old,
and she said, "Mom, there's a hair sticking out
of your chin." I glanced in the rearview mirror
and said, "Where? I don't see it." Then she
said, "No. Look on your other chin."

—Mimi, 42

54

It's easy to look in the mirror and obsess
about the changing face of our lives.
It's more challenging to get still enough
to listen and understand what
the God Who Never Changes
is trying to say to us through it.

Midlife issues can help us sort through what's important. They have the power to say, "There's a pretty good chance you've already used up more than half the days you're scheduled for. So be all the more vigilant not to squander the rest."

I'm not terribly moody, but I do find that I feel anxious at times. That's new for me. Sometimes I lie in bed at night and realize I feel anxious, but I'm not sure why. I do worry sometimes about something happening to my kids, like injury or death.

—Anne, 48

Anti-Insomnia Tips

- Avoid caffeine late in the afternoon and evening.

- Eat heavier meals early in the day and lighter meals in the evening.

- If you must snack at night, try things like turkey, tuna, bananas, or milk. They contain tryptophan, which can help you relax.

- Avoid vigorous exercise or stimulating TV programs at least one hour before bedtime.

I will lie down and sleep in peace, for you alone, · · ·

- Take a hot shower or a warm bath with Epsom salts. (Magnesium relaxes the muscles.)

- While preparing for bed, listen to soft music and avoid bright lights.

- Pray about issues that are causing you anxiety, stress, or fear.

... O LORD, make me dwell in safety. —Psalm 4:8

My biggest fears are about things like totally losing my memory, female organs dropping, not being attractive enough to keep my husband's interest. I don't want to be old and feeble and too weak to pick things up.

—Shirley, 40

60

Taking the time to sit down
and admit our random fears in writing is
one way we can shine a flashlight
in their eyes and force them
to come out with their hands up.

Some of us experience an increase
of unexplained anxiety when our hormones
rise or fall. We may not realize that a fear
is hormonally related when we're in the
middle of it; but if we look back later,
we can see the pattern.

The best antidote for fear is not

something *we do* as much

as it is something *God has done*.

As a parent, I'm closer to my kids now that they're young adults. It's great to sit back and enjoy the fruit of all your hard work in raising them. But not having them at home to create all that excitement and enthusiasm leaves a void.

—Mary Lou, 51

A middle-aged mom needs a safe place
to land if she happens to struggle now
and then with the process of dismantling
the home and family she has spent
decades—at great personal expense
and exhaustion—to construct.

When a woman has laid down her life
and fought for her family spiritually,
physically, emotionally, and financially
and has given the very best years
of her life to them, she deserves patience,
understanding, and applause—
not being told, "Just get over it."

Grace is what we need to be bathed in
every day in this season of our lives.
Because even though no one is dying,
sometimes it sure feels like it.

Getting a Grip
on Your Empty Nest

Idea #1: Invite older, godly women to share their insights with you about parenting adult children. Ask:

• How hard was the transition out of hands-on motherhood for you?

• What mistakes did you make? What things are you glad you did?

Delight yourself in the LORD and he will . . .

Idea #2: Start a Fresh Empty Nesters group. Discuss questions such as . . .

- What makes you most sad about your children leaving home? What are the "upsides"?

- Are you finding ways to be an encouragement to your grown children without getting overly involved in their lives?

. . . give you the desires of your heart. —Psalm 37:4

Among the many unsettling parts of middle age is the feeling that the important people in your life are sneaking off to a fun spot and you're not invited. We sense a mass exodus at two significant relational poles: Our kids exit stage left, while our parents exit stage right.

*My daughters and I relate more as friends
now. We love doing things together. But it can
be confusing trying to figure out when to step
in and when to stay out of their lives. It's a
stretch for a "fix everything" mom
to let them become adults.*

—Martha, 49

71

We're referred to as the sandwich
generation because we find ourselves smack
in the middle—and stretched beyond all
recognition by the tension—
of caring for our kids and our parents.

I feel like I've become the parent and my
mother the child. Both my brothers
live in other countries, so I'm it for my mom.
That can be suffocating at times.

—Anne, 48

As we've gotten older, our parents have
gotten even older than the "old"
we used to think they were when we
thought we knew everything.
This can be one of the
scariest revelations in life.

When I feel good and the grandchildren are
behaving, being a grandma is the sweetest thing
in the world. I have as much love for them as I
do for my very own. But on the other days,
I'm so glad I can send them home.

—Lisa, 47

75

Any number of extra-raw
parent-child/child-parent emotions are
bound to surface in middle age, and the
healthiest way to deal with the little
monsters (the emotions, not the children)
is to herd them all out into the daylight,
where we can get a good look at them.

I'm expecting our fifth baby any day.
I thought I was done having babies, but then
God began to tug at my heart. For two years
I argued with Him: "God, You couldn't
possibly mean to start all over again."
But He did. Following God
is anything but boring!

—Lindsey, 41

77

Dear Jesus,

The further I get in this unique time in my life, the more I see what a radical passage it is. I need Your help. You knew the conflicting emotions of taking up Your cross and redirecting Your mother's love from Yourself to someone else. I can relate in a small way to that conflict and to the call of the bigger picture. So I pray for the growing cooperation on my part with every directive passed down from the "home office." Help me to be strengthened by the changes I'm going through rather than paralyzed by them, and to accept the plan You have set before me.

I wasn't prepared for midlife. I didn't read or prepare mentally for personal and family changes. But I like my age now. I feel I've experienced a number of things—like travel, education, and faith—that keep me looking forward and moving ahead.

—Mary Lou, 51

80

Whatever our take on empty nest syndrome, the wisest among us say to ourselves, "This is your time . . . see the possibilities . . . seek new ways to fill the gaps . . . put to fresh use your previously spoken-for finances . . . spend your energy on people and things that will last."

If skydiving, parasailing, or the latest
parachute-wearing sport
is something that really piques your
interest—get your heart and head
examined first. Then go for it.

Reading is like sit-ups for the brain;
according to the experts,
it's exactly the kind of exercise
people need as they mature.

Writing your memories is not only a great pastime, it's a great way to trace the grace of God in your life and give testimony to the next generations of the power of Christ to change and sustain those who follow Him.

A lot of women change jobs, start small businesses, or find creative ways to alter their job descriptions at midlife. Some of us will work less, while others will work more. Do whatever works for you.

When you find yourself thinking, *Someone really needs to do something about that*, perhaps that's the Holy Spirit prompting you—to birth through you a new way of caring for the people God loves.

As the echoes from our empty homes trail off, we need to take the quickest, most proven way back to purpose and joy in life: finding new, fulfilling ways to open our hearts—and then, one little piece at a time, giving them away.

A Ralston Purina company survey
revealed that 57 percent of pet owners
were forty years old or above.
And 60 percent of the pet owners surveyed
had no children under eighteen in the
house. Which means if you don't own a
pet, you can expect a strange
hankering for one soon.

*Although the decision to purchase Sophie,
our teacup poodle, was made on a whim, I had
been aware for some time that our family
dynamics could change any minute.
Within a few months, our oldest daughter
was engaged. The exodus is beginning.
But Sophie will stay here with me.*

—Lauren, 44

89

10 Things You Should
Know by Now

1. How to make a small room look larger

2. How to make a large woman look smaller

3. How to love the woman God made you to be

4. Your three greatest strengths

5. Your top three weaknesses and how to not be limited by them

6. How to get away for a couple of nights, alone, without fear that your husband, kids, or Foo-Foo the cat will starve to death

I know that you can do all things; . . .

90

7. What year your money-market account will finally amount to something

8. How to let your adult child make her own decisions without pitching a fit, resorting to pills, or pigging out in the pantry

9. How to make a genuine connection with God

10. That joy does not need a reason

. . . no plan of yours can be thwarted. —Job 42:2

There's a reason people talk about the
midlife crisis. As our age increases,
we become like pots that have simmered
on the stove too long. Sometimes
the lid blows off.

I try to surround myself with other women
who are going through the same things.
We laugh and cry together. I try to take care of
myself, pamper myself once in a while.
For me, a good haircut really helps.

—Laurie, 37

93

The Bible says a lot of great things about keeping a positive attitude. We're encouraged to rejoice and be glad. But sometimes, at certain significant crossings in life, the most profitable, productive, proactive thing a girl can do is to have a good cry. And the Bible encourages that too.

Most of us come from a long line
of stiff-upper-lip, crying-will-get-you-
nowhere sentiments. And while intended
to make us strong, this kind of thinking
may actually block us from experiencing
the depth of emotional healing that can
come from "constructive complaint."

My biggest midlife challenge was a deep
depression, but I didn't recognize it as such.
I stopped going to church, didn't get out of bed.
My husband just thought I had gotten lazy all
of a sudden! I tell women to get help.
Talk to other women and to doctors.

—Grace, 67

Midlife should be all about forging
ahead, blazing new trails. But in the
process, many of us can expect to
experience, to varying degrees,
one or more authentic stages of grief,
including feelings of denial, anger,
isolation, and despair.

We all process change at different rates
and depths, and no two people
will mourn the passing of the first stage
of adulthood the same way.

The best gift we can give our midlifing
comrades (and ourselves) is
permission to embrace this
new season by first spending some
time in sorrow.

Carve out quality time for some good grief. If it's done purposefully and honestly, in the presence of the Holy Spirit and perhaps a few friends, our efforts to say a heartfelt good-bye to what was might make saying hello to what's next that much easier—and no doubt sweeter.

My eyesight is going. I have jiggly arms, and my legs look like a bad case of pudding. It amazes me that my husband still thinks I'm beautiful. At year twenty our marriage turned a corner—it was like everything clicked, and the last eight years have been the best ever.

—Susan, 49

101

Midlife Survival Guide

1. Keep moving.

2. Be often among safe, caring womenfolk.

3. Look in the mirror and say, "[Your name], you are beautiful, grace filled, and priceless to God."

4. Buy new athletic shoes. You'll walk faster and jump higher.

5. Find creative ways to be near water. Jesus did.

6. You already know about sunscreen.

My grace is sufficient for you, for my . . .

7. Discover the elegance of three-quarter-length sleeves.

8. Stoke your private devotions. Recite meaningful scriptures. Pray aloud. Create your own worship songs.

9. Tell your troubles to Jesus. Dump the whole truck in His lap. He can take it.

10. Embrace the wow of now. Rejoice in all its fresh, sweet, juicy possibilities.

. power is made perfect in weakness. —2 Corinthians 12:9

A lot of women don't care much for change. You really can't blame them. Change can be rude. It never says, "Oh dear, sorry for the inconvenience. This will only take a second."

Just as clothing trends often mimic earlier times, so it is with the changing wardrobe of our lives at this halfway point. Many tried-and-true options still work. There are anchor points too, especially if we've asked the Rock of Ages to be the buyer and keeper of our closet.

Lord,

Help me to sleep like a child
through the earthquakes. Help
me to waltz on the shifting sand
and stay loose through the rugged
detours—even those I must take

Great is the LORD and most worthy of praise . . . .

in the dark. May I walk to the lead of Your still, small voice. Let me smile at the rising sun, and may I steer in the night by those stars You have hung just for me.

. . . his greatness no one can fathom. —Psalm 145:3

*The fact that I have a relationship with Christ
keeps me going. Because we walk by faith
and trust, and not by sight and feelings,
I know He is in control. I count on
the healing I find in Him.*

—Lisa, 47

108